i

Memory Improvement
The Secrets of Memory Manipulation Revealed

Memory Improvement

The Secrets of Memory Manipulation Revealed

Retrain Your Brain to Improve Your Memory
and Discover Your Unlimited Memory
Potential

Memory and Learning Exercises to
Remember More

Kyle Faber

Memory Improvement – The Secrets of Memory Manipulation Revealed

Retrain Your Brain to Improve Your Memory and Discover Your Unlimited Memory Potential

Copyright © 2018 Kyle Faber

Published by CAC Publishing LLC.

ISBN 978-1-950010-17-2 paperback

ISBN 978-1-950010-16-5 eBook

Contents

Introduction: An Evolving Memory

Improving your memory isn't just about remembering phone numbers or where you put your keys. By remembering to look after your memory, you can boost the performance of your mind so that more information will be available more quickly, you can make better decisions, and achieve your goals more effectively.

In recent decades, there has been an explosion in our understanding of how the brain works, how memory is encoded and stored, and how much mental capacity we really have. This increase in knowledge has come from two directions. On one side, there are the hard sciences of neuroscience, biology, and genetics. On the other side are the softer sciences of psychology and philosophy. This book balances both.

Memory is not a single thing. We have a variety of types of memory, which can be broadly categorized as *sensory memories*, *short-term memories,* or *long-term memories.* Sensory memory is the shortest lasting memory of all, lasting just fractions of a second, long enough for a sense to process its input. Short-term memory has a very different purpose than long-term memory and is encoded differently in the mind.

Short-term memory is encoded rapidly and is meant to last a short time, less than 30 seconds. Long-term memory takes longer to stitch together but is meant to last indefinitely. If content went directly into long term memory, that memory item would not be available for a few minutes immediately after it occurred as it is being encoded into the long-term memory. Also, there would be no process to filter the important from the unimportant, so we would be overwhelmed with a massive amount of unnecessary memories. Both would result in a very incoherent mental experience.

The first type of long-term memory is *explicit memory* (or *declarative memory*) – which is what we tend to think of when we talk about "memory." It requires conscious thought. It's what we try to specifically store in memory. It's what we are using when someone tells us their date of birth or phone number and we put in the effort to remember the information. Generally, this is the kind of memory people are talking about when they say they want to improve their memory, but there are many other types of memory that are equally important to keep functioning at optimal levels.

A second type of long-term memory is *implicit memory* (or *non-declarative memory*). These are the things we remember automatically, without conscious thought, almost as second nature once learned. *Procedural memory*, remembering how to do a complex activity without conscious attention, is a very common type of implicit memory. Once someone has learned to read, drive a car, or tie shoelaces, through repetition, it becomes procedural memory. *Muscle memory*, or *motor learning*, is a type of procedural memory, and is a huge part of the practical side of memory. Everything from walking on a regular pavement to balancing on a gymnasts' beam, and riding a bike are examples of muscle memory.

There are also memories that have to do with who you are – your *episodic memory* – all your experiences, your name, what you look like, who you are, where you live, who the significant members of your family are, and so on. These are the memories that make up our personal and collective histories.

There are the memories of what we want which keep us moving toward goals, and the memories of what we don't want which remind us to move away from the undesired.

And then there are the memories of hard data, facts, and information that aren't drawn from personal experience, our *semantic memory*. This is most of what we learned in the classroom. This is most of what we know for our professions or our interests. This is our general knowledge of the world and our culture.

Memory is not only the foundation of all of your knowledge, but it is also the center of your social life, it is the core of your profession, and it is the soul of your desire. Without memory, you would not know who that man or woman is that you see in the mirror each morning. You need memory to associate that face in the mirror with a set of values, beliefs, experiences, and relationships with others. You need a great memory to do all that and more.

The evolution of the brain

The brain's evolutionary path has not been one of random mutation and adaptation; it has been one of gradual development driven by internal desires, and by needs triggered by the external environment, and by the challenges presented by our surroundings that we need to overcome to achieve our objectives. The brain's evolution has been largely responsible for humans rising from being third rate scavengers (after the lions and hyenas) in the wild to claiming the pinnacle of the food chain as the dominant species.

Early hominids, who were our ancestors about two million years ago, used to trail lions and hyenas, not to hunt them, but to wait in the shadows to scavenge what was left after they were done with their prey. Bones were all that were usually left, from which they picked the scrapings, but they also began to use those bones as tools.

Those tools helped them expand their capabilities – and that brought them better food. Better food and nutrition allowed the brains of early humans to develop. The more their brains developed, the more powerful the tools they developed, accelerating their rise to the top.

The skull of the man-ape, *Australopithecus*, from two to three million years ago, has a cranial vault that was comparatively tiny – a mere 490 cubic centimeters. A million (or two) years later, *Homo Erectus*, or the Java Man, had a slightly larger cranial vault of about 935 cubic centimeters. Then, just 100,000 years ago, *Homo Sapiens Neanderthalensis*, Neanderthal Man, had a larger cranial vault that measured approximately 1,600 cubic centimeters, even larger than present-day humans. Present day man has a slightly smaller cranial capacity of 1,350 cubic centimeters. The decreased size is the result of the increased efficiency of the modern human brain.

The evolution of memory

Different features and types of memory developed over millions of years, in response to needs that emerged as species evolved. *Spatial memory* came about because early species that had developed ambulatory skills needed to know where they were and where they were going. Spatial memory prevents you from going around in circles, not knowing where you are at any given point in time. It is also crucial to the ability to forage for food and for venturing out into the world to hunt and explore. Spatial memory developed because there was a need for it.

As the brain developed further, other skills and abilities were added to it. *Feature memory* allows us to remember what tree bears what fruit by recognizing the features of the tree. It allows us to remember a location by remembering the features of the surroundings. Feature memory allows us to distinguish one kind of plant from another so that we can realize that, under the ground, a specific plant will have a tasty root vegetable. Memory evolved as was needed for the tasks that were asked of it until we now have the various powerful faculties that we, as a species, take for granted.

Even for an individual, the basis for any mental improvement or memory enhancement is actively pursuing a need or desire that requires it. If you want to memorize phone numbers, but you continue to use your smartphone's contact function to "remember" phone numbers, then you are not really acting on your desires. There isn't really any need to develop the ability to remember those numbers.

As various types of memory developed in response to the needs of early man, two related things were happening in the background. As the brain developed more capabilities, it needed more capacity. As mentioned, the cranial capacity of the early biped humanoids grew bigger, indicating the larger volume of its contents, the brain.

As more memory and processing capabilities became available, a better system for organizing and prioritizing the vast amounts of new data was needed. The brain developed a system of preferential encoding of memory or biased competition. The memories that are encoded for long-term storage and are the most easily accessible are those with the highest need of being retained. There is a sort of competition between individual memories as to which gets encoded. The memory with the strongest bias or emotion is the one that gets more connections during the encoding process and thus has a better chance of being remembered.

In other words, we remember what has aroused and motivated us. Hunger arouses us to remember where to find food, and fear motivates us to remember where to find shelter and to remember what dangers to avoid. Those are powerful basic instincts, and they exert significant control over what we remember and what we forget.

With a system in place to determine what was important to remember, the brain's development leapt forward. That system became the basis of what the brain remembers – and that determined how the species evolved. Imagine if we remembered how to find our cave, but not how to find our prey. Or if we remembered every detail of the shapes of a cloud, but not the face of someone who threatened our safety. What would happen? How the brain knows what to remember has been an important factor in the success of our evolving development.

Our brain selects out as important to remember those memories which are tied to powerful emotions. We tend to remember mistakes more than achievements, and bad events more than good, because that helps to keep us from repeating those. We remember conflict and uncomfortable events because fear is a powerful emotion that marks out situations that are better avoided. It is valuable for us to remember bad experiences and dangerous events, but it can also become debilitating if when we go overboard with that.

If you are like many people and believe you have a bad memory, think again. You don't. You can prove it to yourself just by remembering something bad that happened to you. That proves that your memory circuits are working just fine. You simply need to realize that you are motivated to remember some things but not others.

Understanding that the brain evolved to remember things based on how much they affect you gives you your first tool for expanding your capacity to remember. If you want to increase how much you remember, then you need to be in a state that finds the information you want to remember useful, important, even urgent. So, the first tool to improve your memory is to understand your emotional and mental state, and your motivation for remembering something. You can't expect to remember anything that you are approaching in a half-hearted way. Are you motivated enough to remember it?

Ironically, it is memory, itself, that helps you remember what you are motivated to move toward, whether that's a better memory or some other thing. The ability to remember objectives, *goal memory*, allows you to project what will happen next and move toward it. It allows you to learn from experience, so you can circumvent poor outcomes by having goals that keep you on a track toward outcomes that will make you better off. Goal memory is a powerful tool that the human mind uses to imagine a future and then work toward it. It gives you the ability to think about what to have for lunch before you are hungry. It allows you to plan for summer vacation next year while it is still snowing outside.

It isn't an exaggeration to say that when you take charge of your own memories, improving not only how much you remember but also the quality of the memories you choose to make, you are deciding who you will become moving forward. When a pattern of memories forms, that can determine your frame of mind. Putting all your memories together, you have the basis for your mindset and a personality – and that determines your behavior and the path your future will take.

It really doesn't matter if you don't take the time to remember phone numbers, you can get your phone to do that for you. But you can increase the power of your mind by improving your memory. It is not an exaggeration to say that memory is the key to what becomes of you in your own personal evolution, and that it is one of the keys to your destiny.

Chapter 1: The Brain, Neurons, and Memory

A basic understanding of the physical brain and the lifecycle of neurons provides clues on how to have a robust and effective memory. Over a hundred billion neurons and significantly more glial cells make up the three-pound mass of the brain.

Neurons, which are the primary signaling cells of the human body and brain, range from just a few microns in length inside the folds of the brain to a few feet in length along the spinal column and spreading across the network. These neurons connect to each other – by association, the single most important organizing and operational feature of the brain and memory. Each neuron connects with anywhere from a thousand to tens of thousands of neighboring neurons. *Interneurons*, one of the main types of neurons, form connections between neurons. Interneurons are also known as *association neurons*.

Each neuron that comes into being is useless until it is in place and connected to other neurons. An individual neuron, with its bit of information, only becomes useful when it connects with another neuron that has another bit of information. Each neuron is connected to another neuron across a void called a *synapse* – transmitters need to jump this gap to complete the connection.

A neuron can connect to thousands of other neurons, but that connection is not physical – it is air-gapped – which is a pretty ingenious part of the structure. If the connection were continuous, there would be information flowing everywhere indiscriminately. A continuous connection between neurons would result in an incoherent and useless jumble of noise.

Instead, electrical and chemical signals have to jump across the synaptic gap. A certain threshold of effort must be applied before information is transmitted across that gap. As an electrical impulse moves from the *soma* through the *axon* to the *terminus*, it signals *vesicles* to release *neurotransmitters*. These neurotransmitters leave the *axon terminus* and jump the synaptic gap to the connected neuron.

When neurons "fire," they fire in unison and in sequence. That's why we think of an idea as a moment of illumination – there is literally a light that flashes – and you can see it on an MRI.

On the other hand, a neuron in isolation has the sole purpose of holding a fragment of information – which, by itself, is essentially useless. It's like taking the *Declaration of Independence* and keeping just one letter of the whole document, let's say the "D" from "Declaration." That D, on its own, has no context, could mean anything, and therefore has no real meaning.

In the same way, individual bits of information floating around in your head without context and association are useless, and only take up resources without adding any value. When the bits of information are brought together, context and association give meaning to the information (i.e. memory), narrowing down its purpose and place in the brain. That means that when you want to remember something, try to put it into a context – give each fragment of information "meaning" by anchoring it to something that you already know.

Of course, not all neurons are designed to store fragments of memory. Neurons, in general, are cells that send, receive, and relay electrochemical messages, but there are different types of neurons with different roles. Most neurons in the brain are tasked with performing motor functions, while others perform sensory functions. *Sensory neurons* relay sensory information, and *motor neurons* send signals down the spine to individual muscles and muscle groups to generate action in those muscles. Sensory neurons account for less than one percent of the total neurons available, while motor neurons account for close to ten percent of brain mass.

Overwhelmingly, the rest of the cells of the nervous system and brain are actually non-electrochemical brain cells called *glial cells* that do a lot of support work unrelated to the storage or action potential of neurons. Up to 90 percent of the brain are glial cells. *Glial cells*, or *glia*, do things like digest dead neurons, supply nutrients and oxygen to neurons, manufacture protective sheeting, and help to provide an environment for the flaccid neurons preventing them from tangling with each other. The overall physical health of the brain and memory is tied up with the health and functioning of those glial cells.

Until recently, it was believed that we were born with all the neurons we would ever have in our lifetime, and that when a neuron died it was never replaced. However, it now only beginning to be understood that neurons have a much more complex life cycle than formerly believed. We aren't born with a specific set of neurons that never changes throughout our life, except to die. Rather, some are born, some live, and some die. *Neurogenesis* and *neuroapoptosis* are about the birth and death of neurons. *Neuroplasticity* is about the way neurons change over a lifetime.

The birth of neurons: *neurogenesis*

Neurogenesis refers to the birth of neurons, the foundational circuitry of the brain. The first thing to remember is that you are not born with a full and fixed set of neurons, and you don't spend

23

your life with a predetermined number. It is now understood that new neurons continue to be created throughout life, and that you are not born with all the neurons you would ever have, as was previously believed. Although human babies are born with an enormous number of neurons, and many of those will stay functional until the person dies, there are also new neurons created every day. It has been observed in recent research that there is a special type of stem cell responsible for the birth of new neurons.

For our purposes, though, what is most important to understand is that the birth of new neurons is triggered by what we do, learn, think, and experience. In neurogenesis, cells in the brain respond to the stimuli of learning a new skill or repeating it frequently. When something new is learned, new cells are formed in one part of the brain and then moved to the area of the brain where they are needed. The hippocampus, the area of the brain responsible for consolidating and transferring memory into long-term storage, is also where neurogenesis is found to occur. This generation of new neuronal cells is a lifelong process.

If you want a brain and memory that functions at its best, then you need to make sure to stimulate the birth of new neurons by learning and doing new things. Learn a new language. Do puzzles.

Try something completely new. Your memory will be better for it.

The importance of the brain's capacity to generate new neurons is nowhere more evident than when there has been an injury to the brain. From the perspective of adaptation after injury, neurogenesis is a subset of neuroplasticity. As long as the brain is supplied with the right nutrients, adequate levels of oxygen saturation, and a sufficient supply of blood, neurogenesis can occur even in old age.

For instance, if a stroke victim has damage in the area of the brain that controls walking, repeated practice in re-learning to walk triggers neurogenesis. Those new neurons are moved to the location in the brain involved with the ability to walk, that is, to the location in the brain that "remembers" how to walk.

For an older person, that process of re-learning after a stroke can take significantly longer if there is suboptimal cardiac and pulmonary health, and reduced muscle mass which makes it harder to complete physiotherapy. If all these are overcome, the person can regain the ability to walk, but returning to full pre-stroke gait and strength takes practice and repetition.

Neurogenesis is important for everyone, not just when there is injury or damage. It is central to having a good, optimally functioning memory. Maintaining a good memory is about creating new neurons and new connections, whether that's for new memories or simply keeping old memories alive. If, for any reason, you became unable to trigger neurogenesis, you would not be able to create any new long-term memories from that point forward. And anything new that you learn (or re-learn) would not be available to you.

Once it has been created, the new neuron needs to be moved into its final place. This occurs in a couple of different ways that are still being studied. One way is through the use of chemical signaling. New neurons are guided by adhesion molecules along existing migratory pathways until they get to where they are going. Much of this happens as you asleep, and, as new neurons creep against existing neurons, some may be triggered, causing dreams of the content it has triggered. New neurons may also crawl along radial glia as they migrate to their new sites.

Memory by association is so effective because new neurons don't just materialize to fill in an empty spot – they need to be located near or attached to other neurons. To be attached to another neuron, the information needs to be related. This is why most of the strategies in this book are based on associating a new memory with an old one.

Any given memory has just a one in three chance of getting to its optimal storage location, of being stored in the best place for it to be recalled easily later. This is one of the reasons we have little gaps in our memories, the reason we forget things we feel we should remember easily, and the reason behind much of the confusion we experience.

The implications for improving your memory are clear. You should perfect each memory so that it is not only well formed but it is also more likely to arrive at the best location for it to be stored in. Strategies to accomplish this include everything from paying attention to staying in good health.

The death of neurons: *neuroapoptosis*

Neuroapoptosis is the exact opposite of neurogenesis – it is the death of neurons in the brain, spinal column, or elsewhere in the central nervous system. Cells in the nervous system have unusually long lives, starting at pre-birth, and surviving until death unless there is a serious injury to the brain.

By contrast, other cells in the human body have a lifespan that is shorter than that of the person, living anywhere from just a few days to a few months. Of course, the full potential lifespan of any cell applies only when the body is healthy and under optimal conditions. If there are other factors like suboptimal nutrition, substance abuse, and injury, cells, including neurons, are not likely to live out their full lifespans.

The benefit of having cells that never die is that memories can last a lifetime. The downside is that the cerebral environment, therefore, has not been designed to automatically replace specific cells when they are damaged or die. The only way to generate new neurons is to do new things, travel to new places, experience new sensations. This includes re-learning old things to replace damaged neurons, for example, in the event of a stroke.

Even though most people think that fading memory has to do with the physical attrition of brain cells, this is not usually true. When you forget something, it's not because your brain cell has died. It's because you are not making use of it, so the number of connections that lead to the memory have been reduced to conserve resources. The cells that hold your memories require a lot of energy, oxygen, and nutrients to maintain themselves over their lifespan, so the brain cannot afford to expend resources on memories that are not important enough to be used. So, this means that while the neuron housing the memory may still be alive, the pathways to retrieve the memory may be disappearing.

The living and changing brain: neuroplasticity

Neuroplasticity refers to the brain's ability to physically change throughout life, altering with experiences, learnings, and injuries. The principal way this occurs is through the birth and death of neurons, and the changing connections between neurons.

Every experience you have reverberates throughout the brain and causes changes to it. Your brain is never the same from one day to the next. As Heraclitus said, "A man never steps in the same river twice, the river is never the same, and neither is the man." Heraclitus could as well have said that each new experience that a man encounters changes the makeup and map of his mind.

In the wake of an injury, there are a number of ways that neurons are either replaced or repaired. The replacement method of repair, after the death of a group of neurons, is by re-learning the information that was contained in those neurons. That triggers the birth of new neurons to replace the dead or damaged ones.

The second method utilizes what is most commonly meant by the term "neuroplasticity." In the event of damage, the brain continues to use the old neuron but forms new connections in different locations to the existing neuron. This can only occur if the injury has not fully damaged the neuron and only some of its connections have been affected.

You can think of it in the following way. If you build a city with roads that go from city hall to the mayor's mansion, there will be more than one way to get from one location to the other. If one of the roads were demolished, you could build another one to add to the number of available routes to get from one to the other, in case there were traffic jams or other obstacles. However, if one of the buildings, the mansion or city hall, were destroyed, then an entirely new building would have to be constructed. It wouldn't be enough to pave a new road.

In the same way, if the neuron is not damaged, connections can be made with other neurons to connect to it in faster and more diverse ways. If the neuron, itself, is damaged, an entirely new neuron is needed – and learning (or re-learning) is required for that.

Neuroplasticity helps to keep the brain's thoughts and functions intact when there is damage to neurons. It also allows you to change or override something you have already learned, such as an ingrained habit that you want to change. A good way to change an established habit is to extinguish past connections (through dis-use) and to create new connections through learning and practicing the desired behavior – and that process precisely describes what neuroplasticity is really all about.

The changes described by the term neuroplasticity occur whether you make those changes intentionally or not. As you take in and accumulate new information and experiences, and have different thoughts and feelings, the map of neurons and their connections changes, and that changes your brain.

The process of improving your memory is subject to the degree of fixedness of the neurons and the various structures that make up the functional core of the brain. Some elements are hardwired and are replicated from one generation to the next, while others are there to adapt to current circumstances. You can improve your memory, within those constraints, by working with those areas designed to change.

You can even change how effectively memories form, if you practice and place demands on the brain to increase your ability to remember. "Willing" and "trying" are not enough – you need to do the things that increase your brain's ability to create and transport the new neurons into place, and that create more connections between neurons.

In a real sense, you can make yourself into whoever you choose to be (including someone with well-developed memory and mental processes), because everything that makes up who you are boils down to synaptic connections between neurons, and the memories you create that define who you are.

You can take control of this natural neuroplasticity, and, in turn, the quality of your own memory. You can enhance the process of neurogenesis and increase your memory powers – with the right knowledge and exercises to do it. The more nimble you keep your brain, the easier it is to create synapses between neurons, making more of those connections that are at the very heart of memory by association.

Setting the stage for a better memory

If you just jump in and start messing with the neural connections and the synapses in your brain, you probably won't have much success. As with anything, the first thing you need to do is realize that you have in your own hands the awesome power to make the changes you want. Second, you have to call upon the determination and willpower to take the steps that will accomplish what you want.

Third, you need to believe in the benefits you will gain from changing your brain and improving your memory. The one thing that your subconscious is good at is calculating cost-to-benefit ratios. If you are about to embark on something that appears less worthy compared to what you already have, you will find your subconscious trying to sabotage your efforts internally.

That is one of the reasons people fail at trying to improve or change themselves – they do not believe in what they are doing, and they do not have the facts or a way to prove the benefit to themselves. The currency between your conscious and your subconscious is desire and belief. If you have enough desire and belief, your subconscious will be on board, and will work, behind the scenes, to support your efforts.

There are five specific things you can do to set the stage, to create the best environment, for you to work on having a better memory.

1. Reflect

When you do deep reflection on any subject you are interested in, you are actually triggering activity in the neurons, neuronal pathways, and networks associated with the area you are thinking about. That means that when you reflect on something that you want to change, you are activating that area in your brain. So, when you start to think about what memory does for you, all the reasons you want to improve it, your brain begins to work on that for you, behind the scenes.

2. Identify hindrances

Take some time to identify what blocks you from achieving what you want, a better memory. Is it poor habits, poor nutrition, or constant distraction? Or something else? That will help you to identify where you are at the moment. That will help you plot a path from where you are to where you want to go, and provide you with a direction to take. Sometimes those obstacles are the path – remove them and you find yourself where you want to be.

3. Ask

When you "ask" repeatedly for what you want, your subconscious begins to search through all the things you already know, whether you are aware of it or not, and works on the "problem," looking for a "solution" – for a way to get you what you want. Simply asking for a better memory is a powerful tool, and you should never discount the simple act of asking. You will be surprised by the insights and nudges you may get that'll help you to get that better memory you want.

4. Meditate

Meditating has been proven to put your brain into a malleable and receptive state, a state that promotes neuroplasticity. Meditating will also generally increase the effectiveness of all the things you do to improve your memory.

5. Sleep

A good night's sleep can do wonders for memory. The best sleep comes at the end of a physically active day. This means working out, getting your circulation and breathing pumping. With a vigorous workout, your body releases the right hormones to promote not only deep sleep but also neuron binding.

And remember, before you go to sleep, reflect a little, ask a little, and do a little meditation. That'll set you up with the best conditions for having a better memory.

Chapter 2: The Making of Memories

There are three main processes involved in human memory: encoding, storage (which includes *consolidation*), and retrieval. The retrieval process of memory has its roots in the recording process – you can only remember (retrieve) what has become a lasting memory. That means it is important to understand how memories are formed if you want to have a better memory.

There are three stages in the making of every lasting memory of a real-world event. First, we record sensory input into sensory memory. In a matter of seconds, that is moved into short-term memory. Later, that memory is consolidated and moved into long-term memory. It is possible, if we do it right, to go into the farthest reaches of our mind and find much of what has come across our senses. Normally, though, we only remember what we need to remember.

As many have found, writing things down tends to make it easier to recall something later. The aid to memory doesn't come from writing it down so that it is easier to reference the material later on, but comes about because the act of writing, in itself, tells the brain that the material is "important," and needs to be remembered. The brain will then catalog the memory in a way to make recall easier.

Think about some of the clearest memories you have. Are they good ones – or about things that are disturbing? Why is it that you can only seem to remember the things that have had the greatest impact on you and not the things that are inconsequential?

What we remember is, to a large degree, a function of focus. The brain has the potential to record everything, but only earmarks for remembering what we pay attention to. Because what we pay attention to is determined by the impact it has on us, we remember most readily what has had a significant impact on us.

Just how we remember something is tainted or intensified by the state we were in at the time that the memory was created. It affects how long we will remember it, how easily the memory can be retrieved, and the ways it can be retrieved.

Later, our state of mind as we retrieve the memory is also important. Memories are subject to interpretation as they are recalled and interacted with. Memories are malleable when they have been retrieved. When a memory is returned to "storage," in a process of *re-consolidation,* that memory will have been changed by the state we were in while the memory was recalled, and by more recent experiences or information. That is one of the reasons why the memories of witnesses in court proceedings must be corroborated – and why a good attorney can change a witness' mind about their own memories.

Time is another variable that influences memory. Things change in the mind with the passage of time, partly due to ongoing changes in the connections between neurons as new data continues to come in, and partly due to changes in the neurochemistry of the brain as we age.

When an event is perceived, it is encoded as a lasting memory in a series of steps. First, the input is interpreted as sensory data in the relevant sensory cortices. For example, when you see something, the visual stimuli is received by the *visual cortex*, and a memory of the object you saw is created. That memory lasts just long enough – often fractions of a second – as an *iconic memory* in the visual cortex to provide for continuity of visual data. That slight persistence of the image is necessary for us to make sense of our world, for example, to notice that a specific object in our visual field has moved.

The visual data is then sent on to short-term memory, which is part of the larger organizational construct of *working memory* (which overlaps both short-term and long-term memory). Attention to the specific sensory stimuli acts like a filter, selecting out what is sent on to short-term memory.

With more filtering for relevance and importance, some memories are sent on from short-term memory to the *hippocampus* for consolidation with other memories and long-term storage. Each type of sensory data is stored long-term in the sensory cortex that originated it, but now marked out by the hippocampus as belonging with memories in other storage locations. In this way, sight, sound, touch, smell, and other memories "know" to activate simultaneously to produce a complete memory when the memory of an "event" is retrieved.

In the process of forming long-term sensory memories, there are three opportunities to forget. If you are overwhelmed with too much visual data coming in and accumulating in the visual cortex before being sent on to the next step in the process, there will be a loss of visual data. This can result in gaps in the memory and in mistaken sequences of data being sent from the visual cortex to the hippocampus. That's the first memory glitch.

The second opportunity for memory loss is during the actual transmission of the data between the visual cortex and the hippocampus. That loss of data can be the result of degraded synapses or injury. Aging can play a significant role in both.

The third opportunity to forget arises when the hippocampus attempts to connect the data with the input of other senses. When the data is incorrectly matched up, the logic circuits of the hippocampus are likely to reject that memory. What you end up remembering is a lot of confusion instead of the actual event itself.

When SWAT teams enter a hostile location, such as breaking through the doors of a felon's hideout, they make use of this capacity for the brain to become overwhelmed and confused. They come in fast and hard with smoke bombs and loud explosions (harmless, of course). They do this to deliberately overwhelm the senses of the unsuspecting occupant. In the debilitating confusion that ensues, the officers can swoop in and take control of the situation and anyone in it.

When the hippocampus has too many things coming at it, it trips a cognitive circuit breaker and stops processing. It's a way to keep the conscious part of the brain from grinding to a halt. That results in gaps in memory, or areas where the memory hasn't been strongly encoded, causing a rapid degradation of the memory (we call it forgetting), or in incorrect remembering. A simple way to avoid this is to stay underwhelmed. In a world that is going at breakneck speed, it seems almost impossible to slow the information coming at us down, but it is possible.

Short-term memories are those memories stored before being sent to the hippocampus for binding for long-term storage. Although filtered by attention, short-term memories, when they can be retrieved, can be more accurate, not yet having been subjected to the same level of interpretation or bias as occurs with long-term memories. Memories that have been transferred into long-term storage by the hippocampus are not just stitched together and associated with other "relevant" memories, they are also bound by neurotransmitters, such as dopamine, oxytocin, and epinephrine, which chemically mark and "color" the memory as "good" or "bad."

Individual long-term sensory memories are stored in the sensory cortices from whence they originated, after the hippocampus has created connections between them and any related memories. Those connections instruct them to activate simultaneously when retrieved later, forming the complete long-term memory.

It takes lots of practice to be able to extract these memories on demand, but it is one of the ways that competitive memory athletes memorize large volumes of data that they then regurgitate accurately. The best way to develop the ability to recall memories from the visual cortex is to train with flash cards. Flashcard training develops the holding capacity of the visual cortex to accommodate larger amounts of visual data, with more robust connections.

Photographic memory

We can't really talk about visual memory without talking about "photographic memory."

In popular culture, the term "photographic memory" is used to describe a camera-like, mythic ability to capture almost instantaneously the memory of a picture or an image in exact detail and composition and to recall it as a perfect replica indefinitely, calling it up like a slide that one can study. That sort of ability is just that, a myth, promoted by entertaining movies and books.

However, there is real "photographic memory," which is very useful, although it is not nearly so dramatic as the stories would have you believe. Real photographic memory is simply the ability to remember visual images or information in great detail.

When we think of photographic memory, we are typically thinking of visual memory, stored in the visual cortex. But photographic memory isn't the exclusive domain of the ocular sense. There are five kinds of photographic memories, each emanating from a different sensory cortex, visual, auditory, and so on.

Photographic memory can exist in the same way for the other four senses as well. It is possible to remember the sequence of sound exactly as it was heard. Someone like Beethoven or Mozart could recreate the exact sound of what they had heard, even playing with it in their minds before reproducing the sounds with a musical instrument. That is a type of photographic memory too, only for hearing.

A person can develop photographic memory as it relates to visual events, or a highly accurate sound memory, or accurate memories based on any of the other senses or combination of senses.

While many people use the phrases "eidetic memory" and "photographic memory" interchangeably, they are not, in fact, the same thing. *Eidetic memory* is the ability to capture a faithful mental snapshot of a sensory event after only a few exposures and to recall it vividly with precision without the help of memory devices or *mnemonics* for some very short time after exposure. Eidetic memory can apply to visual memory or to the other senses. Eidetic memory is rare, something you were either born with or you weren't, and is believed to be found only in children.

In the end, the difference between a photographic memory and a normal memory is one of degree more than it is of kind. It is possible to develop the ability to recall more, because the human brain is built with the capacity to remember more. However, to conserve energy for survival purposes, the brain only records and recalls events it has reason to believe that we need to remember in order to survive. That is one of the reasons that we remember things that threaten our existence more than we remember mundane events or objects.

Memory encoding

The process of encoding memories begins when our senses capture the various stimuli we experience. Each sense we have – sight, sound, smell, taste, and touch – captures packets of information and sends that on to the cortex associated with that particular sense.

Specifically, visual information detected by the eyes is sent to the visual cortex. Sound vibrations detected by the ears are sent to the primary auditory cortex. In a similar fashion, touch, smell and taste data are sent to the sense's corresponding cortex in different parts of the brain.

Those sensory processing regions are located in different areas of the brain for safety. An injury to a specific part of the head might cause a person to lose their eyesight, but their hearing could remain intact, because it is in a different part of the brain. Imagine if data from all the senses were processed in the same place. An injury to that spot would render the person without any sensory input whatsoever.

It should be noted that not all types of memories go through the same process. For example, implicit motor memories do not need the hippocampus for their transfer into long-term memory. Those who have had damage to the hippocampus or have had the hippocampus removed can still learn and remember new motor skills even while they are unable to remember how they learned it, and they aren't able to form any other kind of new long-term memory.

All the different types of sensory data arising from an event don't immediately "sync up" in the brain. Sensory data taken in by the sensory organs is transmitted to the relevant cortices at varying times. In particular, light and sound travel at different speeds. Think about that for a second.

Let's say there is an explosion a thousand yards from where you stand. That explosion generates light, sound, heat, tremors, and smell. Each type of data travels at a different speed. Light travels significantly faster than sound. The light from the detonation will be the first thing to reach the observer, so that is detected first by the eyes. The next to arrive is the sound, faster than any prevailing wind could carry the smell of the ignition material. Finally, the tremor underfoot arrives as the vibration takes time to move through hard material.

The various sensory stimuli from one single event arrive at the observer's different sensors at different times and is therefore recorded by each sensory cortex at different times.

The data from the individual channels is then sent to the brain's hippocampus where the different sensory memories are stitched together into one coherent virtual event. But to do that, the hippocampus needs to recognize all these events as the same event, even though they arrived at different times from different sources. So, the hippocampus accounts for that and holds on to the event in a kind of subconscious memory as all the data is brought together and assembled.

Once you have recorded everything into memory, the next question will be whether you can recall them all and in the correct sequence.

Now, for a moment, let's think of a sports photographer as an analogy. A sports photographer has some really nifty cameras that can capture hundreds or thousands of frames per second. (The world's fastest camera records over 4 trillion frames per second.) When the photographer is taking pictures of a Formula One race, the event consumes thousands of captures. The shutter release button is pressed and thousands of images are captured in just a few seconds. Imagine taking pictures just as a car starts to negotiate a hairpin turn until the car pulls out of the turn – how many ever-so-slightly-different images could there be?

Sporting event photographers take their pictures like this for two reasons. First, they are ready for any mishap or unexpected event that may happen, and they won't miss that vital shot. Second, it provides a bank of a thousand images, and they can pick the best of the lot. Out of a thousand captured frames, it is certain that at least one picture will be perfect enough to hang the moment on.

When the photographer returns to the studio, all the images are laid out and scrolled through to find the best one. The rest are dropped into an archive or just deleted if they are totally irrelevant. Keeping all those unnecessary photos consumes resources. In photography, gigabytes and exabytes of data cost money to maintain in storage.

Like the sports photographer, the senses record thousands of bits of sensory data, thousands of images, for instance. In the brain, storing a unit of memory uses energy, regardless of whether the memory is active or dormant. Just as the photographer goes through the cache of images and chooses what to keep, the brain cycles through the large amounts of data it accumulates during the course of a day, and then encodes for long-term storage the memories it is programmed to keep.

The memory marked out as "important" will get more connections in the brain, while the memory that is not so important will get less. The more neuronal connections the brain makes for a particular memory, the easier the recall process and the longer the memory stays in conscious recall. Memories that are not considered important are still there, but the synaptic paths to get to them are fewer. Deeper thinking is needed to gradually pull those out of storage.

Now let's take this analogy one step further.

Imagine the same Formula One photographer with thousands of images taken at the event. Going through the image cache for the day, the goal may be to find a particular shot that captured a crash, or an image of a particular driver negotiating a bend. Going through the images intent on finding something particular creates a sort of bias. All else is less important. When one is found that tallies with that bias, it is chosen.

Our memory operates in the same way. If we have a certain bias, the memories we keep will be encoded into long-term memory with that bias. We don't just store the raw memory, we store our interpretation of that memory, an interpretation based on our bias.

So, when we look more closely, we start to see that what appears to be a single event is not really the smallest denomination of a memory packet. We see that memory is made up of multiple streams of information stitched together, and that the memory of one event is built one layer at a time from a mosaic of different events.

Those recalled events are virtual, not physical. Think about that for a minute. We get so caught up with reality and our memories of it that we sometimes think that they are one and the same, or that one is the exact representation of the other. With this, we aren't even talking about confusing fantasy and real events. We are just talking about memory, what we remember. We think of it as "real." It is not. It's not even accurate.

Prior memories dictate how we evaluate newer events, how they are interpreted and stored. This is a process that advances forward continuously. All this is done in the hippocampus, where memories are stitched together. When we go to sleep at night, those memories are then permanently recorded in a bioelectrical process of creating neurons and pathways.

No memory exists in a vacuum. This is where any attempt to compare a human memory to a computer hard drive reaches an abrupt limit. While each memory on a hard drive is recorded in a specific address, and that address is recorded in a registry, the human mind places a neuron in the brain, and then connects that neuron to a network of other neurons based on their associative value. Every single neuron can have anywhere from a few to several hundred thousand connections. The more connections, the more entrenched the memory. On a computer hard drive, a memory either exists or it does not, whereas in the human brain, memory exists in degrees.

Chapter 3: Visualization

What it all comes down to is that the mind has its own virtual reality theater, converting what we observe in the real world into virtual representations. A good way to think about this is to compare it with a virtual reality projection. Imagine donning a pair of VR goggles and finding yourself transported into an environment that is not physical in any way, one that is purely light and sound manipulated by software in a hard drive.

In the mind, things are not that much different. We experience things based on our senses, on what we can observe within the limited ranges of electromagnetic radiation we call visible light, of mechanical vibrations we call sound, and of the scents, tastes, and physical sensations that we have receptors for. There is so much more that we are not capable of detecting, yet we remain convinced that what we perceive is the world and that that's all there is.

So, from those limited ranges of sense perceptions, our mind replicates what it has perceived in the real world as a scene in our mind, visualizing our environment. The reason that we are so easily fooled when a reasonably robust virtual reality scenario is placed in front of us is that a VR system only needs to fool our five limited senses. Once it does that, we "believe" what is presented to us.

What does this have to do with memorization?

The primary tool for remembering is visualization. This is not the same kind of "visualization" we usually talk about when we want to achieve something or the kind a star quarterback might use to "see" the touchdown zone in his head as he huddles before the next play. The visualization we are referring to is the way your mind can place the elements of an environment into a virtual space in your mind.

The beauty of visualization is that it works in both directions. You can either see it in the physical world, then recreate it in the virtual world of the mind. Or you can imagine it in your mind, then work to recreate it in the real world – but that is a topic for a different book.

Memory is an integral part of this visualization, and, conversely, visualization is critical to memory.

There is a virtual "you" in your virtual world, with your body, thoughts, and aspirations all part of that intricate virtual world. Everything you do in the real world is intimately connected with what happens in the virtual world.

To illustrate just how important that virtual world is, think back to a time when you were placed in an unfamiliar situation. Can you remember how you felt? Do you remember the strangeness you felt? That sensation of strangeness that comes from being in a new place forces you to look around and quickly assimilate what is out there in order to build up a virtual version of it as quickly as possible, one that you can use to analyze and interact with the world outside.

To drive home the point, now consider an opposite sort of example. Think about the way you feel in a place you are always in. You become complacent. You are so certain of your surroundings that you don't even need to look at things to know what the room looks like and that everything is in place. When you drive to work along a familiar route, you can do it habitually, almost without consciously thinking about every turn – or even actually remembering how you got to the destination.

But what happens when something new is introduced into the real world unbeknownst to you? You may not even see it. There are two kinds of people, the ones who notice even the slightest change in the room, and others who float through their surroundings, not realizing even the largest alterations. The average person has experienced both.

We have varying thresholds for when a change in real environment shakes us out of our reliance on the virtual (remembered) world in our head and forces us to look outside and adjust the internal virtual view. An obsessive person with a rigidly established virtual world may experience terrible anxiety at changes to their real environment, when the real and virtual worlds no longer match.

Once we realize that we have these kinds of virtual environments in our mind, we can start to use them to place stuff into them deliberately. A new memory that is placed into an existing virtual environment (existing memory) will last longer than it would without a place to reside.

To strengthen your ability to visualize environments, start to make a habit of observing your virtual space and your physical space. This takes concentration and the ability to pay attention. Visualize the places you are in, or places that you usually go to, just as you would see them in a Google street view. Look from a bird's eye view then pan down to the street view and look around.

There are many ways to use the brain's natural capacity for visualization and virtualization to strengthen your memory.

Imagine someone giving you directions on the phone, but you don't have a pen and paper to jot it down. How would you remember it? If you are familiar with the place, then you can just mentally imagine the path to the place you need to go to. But what if you are new to the area and you have no idea what the layout of the city is like? You are not going to be able to visualize a map of the area to mentally follow along the path to your destination.

Instead, you can remember the directions by imagining a place you already know, then asking the person who is giving you directions to tell it to you in terms of when to turn left or right. It will be something like "Take the first left, then the third right, followed by the second left." You get the idea.

As you listen to the directions, instead of trying to imagine the area that you do not know, imagine you are in a place that you do know very well. Imagine standing in a familiar spot in your neighborhood. Let's say, you're on the street in front of your house. Now, imagine if you followed the same directions, first left, third right, and second left. Where would that put you in your neighborhood? Can you visualize it? Now you will know exactly where to go – you will be able to remember the path.

Even if you forget the directions, all you'd need to do is think back to how you would get from the familiar spot in your neighborhood to that destination that you are familiar with. Easy.

This simple example demonstrates the technique of taking the unknown and superimposing it onto something that is known in order to remember it more easily.

You can use the same overlapping technique for a different kind of visualization trick you can use to remember numbers, including phone numbers. If you need to remember a number just visualize a typical keypad. The first row, from left to right, are the numbers one, two, and three. The second row is four, five, and six. The third row is seven, eight, and nine. Finally, the zero is in the center of the last row.

To remember a number like 246, just draw the shape the number makes on the keypad. In this case, it makes an inverted triangle starting at 2.

If you have a number like 212-555-2406, can you picture what that would look like if you traced over the number with your finger? The moment you can use your virtual space to trace out this number, you will remember it. You can see your finger dance back and forth for 212, followed by 555 smack in the middle of the keypad. Then 2406 makes a rectangle from 2 to 4, to 0, then back up to 6. Can you see that? The moment you do that, the path your finger traces across the keypad instantly causes you to remember the number in your virtual space.

The idea of visualization is to take something you need to remember and attach it to something that you already have in your mind, an existing memory. That instantly creates a memory and sorts it for recall. The connection between the old and new memory needs to make sense as an association to your brain, not to you. So long as you provide a path to go from A to B, your mind will make the trip.

Visualization works both in memorization and in retrieving memories. Visualization helps both in the recording or encoding of memories, and in their recall.

Chapter 4: Memory Pegs

Human memory is fundamentally associative. Its robustness and flexibility is grounded in the way that new memories are hooked up with older memories. One memory is connected to another and another and another.

Most of what we do and remember is tagged to other things we do and remember. If you see a brown shoe, you will instantly tag it with the color "brown" and the object "shoe." That can trigger a host of other memories. Perhaps your brother owned a favorite brown shoe, which makes you remember the hairstyle your brother had, and that, in turn, reminds you of *The Brady Bunch*. You started with a brown shoe and next thing you know you've travelled down memory lane to *The Brady Bunch*.

That's the "monkey in the brain" doing its thing. Leaping from one branch of memory to another, according to a vast network of associations. You have to love it because it opens up whole new universes, and it allows you to do things that build on what you already know. While it can be a distraction, it is also an asset.

The brain's naturally capacity for association can be used to help you do some rudimentary tasks like remembering numbers and names. Earlier in the book, we described a way to remember phone numbers using the visualization of a keypad. Now, we are going to remember numbers using an auditory association technique. You will be using common easily pronounceable sounds to represent the numbers.

1 = ono (pronounced oh no)

2 = tot

3 = ere (pronounced hey ray)

4 = fof

5 = afa

6 = sis

7 = asa

8 = tat

9 = ana

0 = oh

Here is how you memorize that – in groups of three.

ono tot ere

fof afa sis

asa tat ana

oh

It almost has a lyrical feel to it, which is what makes it easy to remember. Say that a few times, and you will start to be able to visualize the number that each word represents.

Now look at this number: 246.

But, do not call it two, four, and six. Instead, call it, "tot fof sis." All you need to remember is "tot fof sis."

Short numbers are okay, but the benefits become much more obvious when you apply this technique to a long number.

Try it with this one: 337590729.

"Ere ere asa afa ana oh asa tot ana."

Repeat that a few times, and you will find that you remember it much more easily than the numbers themselves.

The reason this works is that the mind not only remembers audio information faster than visual information, it is also more adept at remembering sounds that rhyme or that have vowel-based syllables. In the days of oral history, before the invention of the printing press, ancient orators and storytellers knew this, so when they needed to remember long, long passages, they did it in poetry.

Favorite tunes have been used with children as an auditory pegging device. When a catchy tune that is familiar, while the words are not, is used, new words can be created for material they need to remember. This is a pegging mechanism where you attach the thing you are not familiar with onto the thing that you are already know. So, in this mnemonic device, the tune is familiar, but the words aren't, and when you put them together, it helps you to remember the new words.

More commonly, however, visual pegs are used to attach the things you have just observed to the things you know very well. Making the association allows you to create a permanent memory of the new observation within moments of observing it.

For instance, you can remember phone numbers by pegging them to a phone keypad. Most phone keypads have alphabets grouped to numbers. This can be used to easily remember a phone number. Imagine trying to remember this number, 1-800-287-86637 (not a real number). Can you remember it? If you use the keypad peg, what you get is 1-800-CUS-TOMER. Which is easier? Companies often get phone numbers that can be remembered this way. After all, how effective would a billboard be if they sold you on a product in the three seconds it took to drive past it, but you weren't able to remember their phone number?

So, memory pegs work. You just need to experiment to discover how it works best for you. A little ingenuity goes a long way here. The basic idea is to peg the unknown onto something you know well. By attaching it to an established memory, there is always a way to remember something new.

That is also the essence of how we remember new concepts and how we acquire new knowledge. When you learn something new, you begin by associating names with things. Then you associate the new process to a process that you already know – using analogies and similes. Once that first layer of learning is accomplished, you move on to the next layer, pegging the second layer onto the first. In this way, you gradually build up a block of information in an organized way.

If you combine this sort of pegging with other techniques that keep your mind calm and free of distraction, you will absorb and remember the data better. Although it is the associative qualities of the monkey mind that make memory pegs work, the memory pegs work better when your monkey mind is brought under control.

Memory pegs are easy to use for less important memory tasks like remembering an address for a few moments until you can get to a memo pad or the note app on your phone. There are many ways to do this. You could hang numbers onto the alphabet, associating a word with the number you want to remember. You could add words to a shape to remember the word through the shape.

Suppose you want to remember the address "147 Airport Rd." Start with an easy way to remember 147 just by visualizing it on a keypad as a straight line from top left to bottom left. (Picture the keypad and where the numbers 1, 4, and 7 are located). Then think of an airport you are familiar with. So, all you need to remember is the straight line on the keypad and the airport – and there you have the address. Don't be surprised if you never forget it again.

It takes a little practice at first, but you will get the hang of it. Your mind will adapt to doing things like this as second nature after just a few attempts, because it is your mind's natural way to learn.

Just as you can peg concepts and numbers to familiar memories, you can remember names of people and faces using similar strategies.

The most important thing about a person's name is that it needs to be "attached" to their face. When we say we want to remember names what we really mean is that we want to be able to associate a name with a face. Think about that for a minute. What is the point of remembering "Bob" (the name Bob) without being able to pick Bob out of a group of people? So, the point, again, is to make an association, to find a way to associate the name with the face.

If the name is difficult to pronounce or you haven't heard it before, and you can't even remember the word, you'll have two tasks to accomplish. One is to learn the name and how to say it, and the second is to associate that name to the face. That's not really a memory storage and retrieval issue so much as it is about knowing the pronunciation and getting a completely new word into memory in the first place. The reason foreign names are so difficult to remember is that you don't have a way to peg it onto something you already know. So, you'll need to approach that in a few steps.

Imagine meeting a fellow named Germapolovitch and learning his name once. The first thing you need to do to is remember to pay attention. Most people don't remember names simply because they are multi-tasking instead of paying attention. You need to stop what you are doing, look directly at the person's face, and listen carefully as the name is pronounced. Germ-a-po-lo-vitch. Pay attention to the different elements of the name, the syllables, the stress points, the intonation.

If you ignore all the surrounding inputs and simply concentrate on the name as the person says it, you will remember the sound in your auditory cortex, while your eyes scan his face, remembering that in your visual cortex. If you continue to pay attention, ignoring all other inputs, your brain will have time to move the data into the hippocampus to stitch the auditory and the visual memories together. If you are also smiling when you meet Germapolovitch, feeling happy, the dopamine released will help to bind the memory. If you are upset when you meet him, that works too, because the epinephrine released will also help bind the memory, although categorizing him in the 'bad column' in your memory.

Another trick for remembering a name is to attach a descriptor to it. "Lying Ted" – remember that one? Or, "Crooked Hillary" – hard to forget once you have heard it. For your personal use, use more positive descriptors. Funny descriptors are okay, but disparaging and negative indicators are bad for you, harming you in the long run – not the other person. The technique, however, is very effective.

All these steps take effort, but that's what having a stronger memory is really about, making the effort to remember. Especially when you need to remember a name, a place, a pronunciation, you need to make the effort before it will "stick," because the brain won't waste resources on remembering trivial or unimportant things. It costs energy to remember. When you make an effort to remember, then you'll find that the brain recognizes that "this is important" and will remember it.

In fact, repetition of names and places (or any other thing you want to remember) is really a substitute for attention and focus. It's the harder way, taking more time and effort. However, if you concentrate on just the one thing you want to remember, and cut out all distractions, both internal and external, you will find that you can remember the thing you need to remember much more easily. Whether it's through repetition, or by simply by paying attention, the brain "gets" that the item is important and should be remembered.

Chapter 5: Memory Palace Method

A little earlier in the book, we described a method for remembering directions, which has similarities to the memory palace method we're about to describe. So, let's review that method of remembering directions by overlaying them onto a familiar mental map.

Mentally start at a place on a mental map you are familiar with, but trace the path from one unfamiliar place to another unfamiliar place, according to the directions someone gives you. When the directions are complete, look to see where you have ended up on your familiar map. Then, all you need to do is remember the destination that you are already familiar with.

For example, suppose you are at a gas station in an unfamiliar town. Your client tells you that you need to turn left as you are coming out of the gas station, make a second left, then turn right at the next intersection, and finally turn left again, and then you will find him at the third house on the left. You have no idea where any of this is, and you can't write it down.

So, as he is describing the directions to you, imagine you are at the gas station near your house. Imagining your own familiar mental map, leave the gas station, take a left. Imagine where that puts you on your familiar mental map, then make the second left, and continue following the directions, but superimposing them onto the familiar terrain in your neighborhood.

Suppose that if you were to follow those directions at home, you would find yourself at the Old Donut Shop. So now you have a starting point, the gas station, and the end point, the Old Donut Shop. You won't need a pen and paper because you know exactly how to get to that point – at home. The scenery may be different, the length of each segment may be different, but the sequence, the intangible process memory, is the same. When you attach that intangible process to an existing memory, you can remember what you need to remember. That is also, in essence, how the memory palace method works, by superimposing the unknown onto the known.

The *memory palace* method, or the *method of loci,* is an ancient Roman and Greek technique taught by orators. It uses the visual memory of a physical location or journey as the framework for hanging other information that you want to remember. It takes advantage of the ease with which visual data can be remembered to help retain other material that may be more difficult to remember. It also takes advantage of spatial memory.

In particular, the memory palace method uses the memory power of association and attaches new memories to buildings and places that you have been to or know very well. This is the same theme again – attaching something unfamiliar to something familiar.

The place you chose for your memory palace has to be somewhere you can navigate in your mind fluently without error. You can use an apartment building, a school library, your campus dorm, any place you have a thorough knowledge of. Leave whatever furniture is there that you remember, but you don't have to focus too much on what was there or what wasn't. As long as you can remember the rooms individually, it doesn't matter whether they are empty or furnished exactly – it's about remembering what strikes you.

I use the Tower of London as one of my memory palaces because I've been there many times. It's one of the most conspicuous structures in London and was where prisoners were brought to be incarcerated. Inside the Tower of London, there are many rooms and cells within a vast network of individual sections – which works very well for me as a memory palace. Over time, you can create as many memory palaces as you can use and remember.

Name the rooms in your memory palace according to the way the room makes you feel, or for something like an ornament that makes the room distinctive. You should be able to remember the name easily. For example, the White House's "China Room" is not about the country, China, but about the porcelain plates that are on display in it. The room is named after what is distinctive about it. Do the same thing with the rooms in your own memory palace. You can name them just by adding a descriptor, Stinky Room, Funky Corridor, Blue Stairwell, or whatever makes sense to you.

Once you have created and named the room in your memory palace, you can use it as a framework for hosting things you need to remember. Walk around this building in your mind. Does the name of the room appear to you instinctively? If it does, then you are ready to take the next step, using your memory palace to remember something.

Memory palaces are particularly good for remembering ordered lists or sequences of directions. Have a consistent path to walk through the palace, with repeatable stations or stops along the way. Identify specific spots that you always visit in the same order. If you want, you can also associate each spot with a number. You will use these locations to hang items that you want to recall. For example, if you have a shopping list of nine items, you could mentally walk through your memory palace, stopping at each location, and creating and focusing on creating a clear mental image of the shopping list item in that spot. It's even better if you can make the image memorable, odd, or funny in some way.

How would you use a memory palace to remember the ingredients and steps to make crème puffs – a fairly easy task to start with?

Start with the ingredients. A quart of milk – in your imagination, mentally picture it at your first stop in whatever memory palace you are using. Next, picture the sugar at the next spot, and so one.

To remember the steps in the recipe, you could visual one step at each location in the right order in the memory palace. The more vivid and interesting that you make the image in your mind, the more effective the mnemonic technique will prove itself to be.

As you go through the memory palace process, maintain a feeling of happiness, thinking of how happy your spouse or child is going to be when you surprise them with this dessert, or imagine how happy you will be as you enjoy eating the finished product. The extra emotional oomph will help to bind the memory faster and for a longer time.

By associating the recipe with a highly familiar locations in your memory palace, you will be able to remember that recipe for a very long time, especially after you have actually done it a few times in your own kitchen in the order you rehearsed in your visualization. The process of physically doing something you visualize solidifies and fortifies the memory, adding more layers of neuronal connections to other parts of the brain, a sort of neuronal redundancy.

Chapter 6: The Neuroplastic Brain

Memory and neuroplasticity

If you want to improve your memory, then you will, of course, be dealing with the brain's *neuroplasticity*. Neuroplasticity is the brain's ability to change physically to adapt to new requirements and new situations. When you embark on a quest to create better memory recall, then you are looking for the brain to demonstrate its capacity for neuroplasticity. Whatever mental and memory limitations you may have experienced, whether from illness, stroke, bad habits or choices, the plasticity of the brain means that you can improve from where you are if you decide to and do what is necessary. The brain is moldable and malleable to the point that even stroke victims can be retaught how to do things, rebuilding what was lost through the death of neurons.

I know an eighty-six year old man who lived a good life until he had a stroke on the left side of his brain. It paralyzed him on the entire right side of his body. If he had been one of those people who gives up, that would have been debilitating, making him homebound, at best, or bedridden, at worse. Instead, within eight months, this man was up and about, getting around, and strolling with his walking stick.

What most people don't realize is that a stroke doesn't kill the muscles in the legs and body, a stroke just kills some of the neurons in the brain that are needed to make walking possible. After a stroke, the part of the brain that controls various aspects of mobility in the affected part of the body have been damaged. But, remember, those neurons are not ones you were born with – the brain created them as you learned to walk. After a stroke, those neurons may be damaged and aren't functioning, but that doesn't have to mean that you will never walk again.

The missing neurons can be rebuilt by learning to walk all over again. Learning creates new neurons that are bound together in a coherent way. When you learned to walk as a child, you built neurons and connections that remembered how to do it. As you practiced, your ability to walk developed further, building on those neuronal networks, and every day you walked during your life, you reinforced and built on those memories of how to walk. Even if those neurons are someday destroyed by a stroke, it doesn't mean that you should accept being paralyzed – it can be possible to gradually create new neurons as you regain your ability to walk.

That is the power of neuroplasticity – a brain that can be changed, improved, and even recuperated after injury. That is the kind of memory that really makes a difference in your life. What you remember, whether deliberately or not, literally alters the contours of your brain. What you decide to do in the physical world can physically alter (for better or worse) your brain as the brain builds new circuits, new connections, and new neurons every day. As long as you have the will and desire to do so, you can influence your own brain functioning by doing new things, having new experiences, and thinking in new directions.

To improve your memory by deliberately working with the brain's own natural neuroplasticity, first, you must want to remember. Then you need to pay attention to what you want to remember. These two things are signals to the brain to do what is needed to help you remember. Do that, if you have a healthy brain, and you will be able to remember anything you want. The rest are just tricks – albeit tricks that can make things a whole lot easier.

As for the man who had the stroke, he had a strong will and no fears of whether he would fail or succeed. He believed in his recovery, and acted on his belief, putting in the effort, and, in a few months, he was back on the sidewalk of life. You can do the same thing when it comes to improving your own memory. You may not have had a stroke, but every one of us has been guilty of neglecting our brain. We abuse our brain with things we eat, what we do, bad patterns in life, and with the things we allow into our mind.

In today's world, the same media that can give you information that builds your mind can give you corrosive material that retards it and your mindset. You can choose. You can be the gatekeeper that decides what your own mind is exposed to and consumes. If you choose wisely, you will be rewarded with a powerful mind that allows you to do more than you can imagine. An enhanced memory is just the start of it.

The brain is a robust organ that can develop new neurons and scaffold off old ones rapidly. We are conceived with flawless memory potential, but we lose it as we get older due to inappropriate nourishment, terrible dietary patterns, poor recreational propensities, substance abuse, and so on. All these things can reduce our unique and powerful capacity to create memories and recall them.

Fortunately, the brain was designed to be neuroplastic, so, if you change your habits and adopt a healthy and positive lifestyle, and you practice remembering, recalling and reviewing memories, you will find that your brain will do that more and more easily. In a manner of speaking, we have all had our own little "strokes." We are, on the whole, patients of absent-mindedness, and have reduced our capacity to do what the brain was originally intended to do –

record and retrieve. But we move our brain functioning, and memory specifically, back to doing what it is fully capable of, and recover from these limitations.

To get anything done, including improving your memory, you need to set a goal. Setting a goal tells your brain to do what is needed to achieve that goal. In this case, the goal would be to work on improving your memory, getting it functioning the way it was intended to and is capable of. When you want it, the doors will open for you, the path will become clear. Everything begins with a goal. No direction and no strategy will emerge if you don't have a clear goal, a clear intention.

Exercise: Write out your intention

Get a notepad and a pen. Put them by your bedside. You can also use a stylus and your tablet to replace the book and pen if you like.

This exercise should be the last thing you do each night before you go to bed.

First, you need your specific goal: I WILL HAVE PERFECT MEMORY.

Then, you need the resolve to do it. You need to set your determination, dedication, and resolve firmly into place: I WILL DO EVERYTHING NECESSARY TO ATTAIN IT.

Your statement is broad, but so certain and set that you are telling yourself that you won't let up until the goal is complete. This is the dedication that will take you to success, regardless of what comes across your path. Regardless of what distracts you, you will return to your goal.

Putting them together, now you get this:

I WILL HAVE PERFECT MEMORY & I WILL DO EVERYTHING NECESSARY TO ATTAIN IT.

Write out this sentence 15 times.

This will keep your goal and the direction you want to go fresh in your mind. You don't have to believe it works, just do it. You will find that the other steps you need to take to enhance your memory will fall into place more automatically. It will keep you on track to a better memory.

Continue writing this sentence out every night, indefinitely.

When you do this, you start to get into "the zone." It gets you geared up. It's the kind of thing a quarterback does to rev up to get into the zone to get a touchdown. There are countless people who have used this "trick" to change their lives. This technique is even better for other types of goals, for careers, better lives, and any kind of self-development. You may find yourself astonished by the way you can get something to materialize just by writing it down.

Unlike other methods in this book for improving memory, this one requires practice and effort. There is no shortcut to practice for building up the skills for a more "photographic" visual memory. This exercise trains your ability to view and "capture" things more quickly, rather than providing a method for memorizing specific material.

For this exercise, use flashcards or an app with a flash card function. Use about a dozen cards for the exercise. Start with cards with simple pictures of objects.

View the cards in rapid-fire sequence. Don't view any card for more than half a second. In other words, flip them at a rate of two cards per second. Never stop to "look" at what is on the card.

You don't want to be consciously trying to analyze and memorize what you see on the car. Your goal is to force your eyes to capture as much as possible in as short a time as possible, without using the verbal and logical parts of your brain.

Have someone hold the cards directly in front of you at eye level. Your focus should be on a point about six inches behind the cards. This will put the face of the card slightly out of focus.

Start flipping the cards. Do not stop even if you think you haven't gotten the information on a card. Just keep going and watch the cards. When you are done, have your partner quiz you on the sequence and content of the cards.

After a few rounds, start using cards with objects with various counts. For instance, the cards may have five balls, four cats, three geese, and so on. The cards should be flashed a little more rapidly this time – at a rate of about three cards per second. Your task is to notice what the object is and how many there are (the count) as the cards are flipped. Once the set is done, you should recall them in the sequence they were shown to you.

Doing these exercises every day will develop your "photographic" memory. You will be more able to quickly see more things in an environment, on a poster, or a person's face – and instantly capture the information that's there.

Exercise: Beethoven's neuron-building *Ninth*

A simple way to increase neurons and the amount of connections between them is to listen to classical music – and not just Mozart. There is no magic to this. Classical music, especially a symphony, has anywhere from 4 to 100 different musical instruments playing in harmony or in several harmonies to create a composite of sound. At first, your ears hear each individual sound, but the mind only "hears" the overall sound – until you train the mind to translate the auditory stimuli as separate instruments. Having "a good ear" isn't about the capabilities of the physical ear, it's about the attention you pay to the sounds. The more attention you pay, the more detail you will hear.

You can take advantage of the inherent qualities of classical music, listening to it as an exercise to build up and develop the connections between neurons and to trigger your brain into making new neurons, so that your capacity to commit material to long-term memory will be greater.

1. Listen to Beethoven's *Ninth Symphony*

Take some time out to really listen to Beethoven's *Ninth Symphony*. The trick is not just to listen to enjoy it, but to close your eyes and wrap a pair of headphones over your ears. Listen to it at a volume sufficient to drown out outside distractions, and listen carefully to the melody. Listen to all four movements in sequence, because the sequence of the music is also part of the overall effect.

(If you ever happen to be in Vienna, try to attend the Vienna Philharmonic to hear the Orchestra perform the *Ninth*. It is an experience that will change you.)

2. Listen to isolate instruments

Listen to the symphony again, in the same way, with a pair of headphones. This time try to isolate the sounds of the different instruments, and the melody each is playing.

3. Listen for subtleties

Listen to the symphony again, this time looking for other sounds you hadn't noticed before. Move your attention away from the obvious sounds you can hear and listen for more subtle ones. You will find, in time, that you will start to hear new instruments. The overall melody will seem completely different after about the tenth time you have listened to it.

Every single time you do this, you will be making new neurons as your brain learns new auditory material, and building new connections between neurons as your brain makes associations with sounds already encoded into its memory.

The act of sitting still listening to a complex piece of music alters your brain forever. Do this every few days for a week, and you will experience the effects of the brain's neuroplasticity as the way that you think, remember, and feel starts to change.

Chapter 7: Emotion & Memory

Emotions are an important part of our human existence and have a profound role to play in memory and mental functioning. Emotions are actually instrumental in creating memories and in determining their longevity.

One of the most powerful signals in the brain that a memory is "important" and should be saved in long-term memory is a strong positive or negative emotion associated with the memory. The stronger the emotion, the stronger the memory will be encoded, with more connections. Memories are encoded by degree of emotional importance, like a ranking scale.

It is commonplace to think of our heart aching when we are deeply troubled. We think of feelings as coming from the chest, and of rational thoughts as coming from our brain, from our head. While these romantic notions are widely accepted, all of our feelings and cognitive thoughts really come from the same place – our brain.

In the same way that the brain manifests hunger in your stomach, the brain manifests emotional discomfort in your chest. The sensations from your stomach don't really come from your stomach – they come from your brain – but it feels like it's your stomach that is calling for food. In the same way, sensations related to feelings and emotions are activated in the chest. Although that has made it into our language and common expressions, when you say things like "My heart aches," or "My heart is swelling," your heart isn't really doing anything.

You can feel anxiety, stress, and worry physically, in your chest and in the tensing of your back. This emotional response is triggered by the release of *epinephrine* (or *adrenalin*), a major cause of the jitters during periods of anxiety. It turns out that one of the key hormones responsible for the creation of long-term memories is epinephrine. It is the triggering of epinephrine during frightening situations that helps to create crystal-clear memories of fear-filled situations.

Now, let's look at this in reverse. If epinephrine is responsible for making strong long-term memories, consider what happens when you take a beta-blocker, a medication that inhibits the uptake of epinephrine. Since beta blockers block epinephrine, the formation of long-term memories can also be affected, and you may start having memory problems. If you are on beta-blockers, you can attest to this side-effect after taking them for some time.

However, if you have been prescribed beta blockers, then you shouldn't stop taking them without consulting your doctor, even if your memory is deteriorating. But if you are not already on beta blockers, then you may want to discuss alternatives with your doctor before taking these kinds of medications.

We especially remember things that cause us immense pleasure or immense pain. In cases of anxiety, epinephrine is released, and a strong memory is formed. On the other hand, memory is also reinforced with the release of *dopamine*, another key *neurotransmitter* in the formation of memories. Dopamine is a powerful "feel good" neurotransmitter that rewards us for doing the activity that triggered its release. Memories encoded with a dopamine release have a happy bias, while ones encoded with an epinephrine release have the opposite tone. We remember immense pain to help us avoid it in the future, while we remember immense pleasure so that we will want to repeat whatever caused it. Remembering pleasure and pain is how the brain manages our experiences.

Oxytocin is another neurotransmitter that is important for memory. Oxytocin, sometimes referred to as the love neurotransmitter, causes us to remember who we love, and even creates that feeling of love. This type of emotional memory is a huge part of our lives. It bonds us with our mates, children, and other family members. It provides the feeling of the assurance we need as we grow up under our parents' protection. It provides strong connections as we form our own communities. Loving emotional memory gives us structure and strength in our social circles, and it contributes to the cohesion we need for a happy society.

Understanding how emotions and neurochemistry strengthens memories and makes them last, you can use this knowledge to design strategies that will result in longer lasting memories when you want to. You can also choose to become more careful about creating negative memories that you might not want to keep or reinforce. For example, you might start to avoid saying or doing anything that escalates a situation when tempers or fears flare. Bad experiences can become emotional baggage, so be careful what you commit to memory.

Emotional memory is powerful, so try not to go down roads that create negative memories that you'll have to deal with in the future. If you are in a situation that is about to turn ugly walk away and save yourself the unpleasantness of carrying that memory around for a long time to come. Reduce your stress, walk away from strife, and learn to calm your mind. This will improve your memory in more ways than you can imagine.

On the other hand, create more good memories, and spend time making memories with those you love and those you want to be close to. Do things in different places and meet new people. All these things will give you the opportunity to make new positive memories. These pleasurable and positive memories will create a better (and more pleasant) cerebral environment for processing and binding memories. If you are happy, more of your memories will be happy too. The momentum of emotional memory created by lots of positive memories will make you a happy person, and you will be more adept at making new positive memories.

Around and round it goes.

The memories held most strongly in our brain help to dictate our emotional reactions, and our emotional reactions help indicate to our brain what we should remember most strongly and clearly. When we understand this cycle, and the cycle is a positive one, we can use that to our advantage to reinforce the things we want to remember. When the cycle is a negative one, we can start to disrupt it, and begin to remember more of what we want to remember.

Chapter 8: Mindfulness, Meditation, and Reflection

Earlier, the way that becoming overwhelmed interferes with memory acquisition was described. Instead, if you can keep yourself from being overwhelmed, the process of transporting memories of events to the hippocampus can occur without a hitch. Information from the various cortices of the brain – each handling data from a different sensory organ – can then be effectively bound together in the hippocampus.

If you can keep the stream of data being processed constant and consistent, then all the parts of the brain, from the cortices to the hippocampus, are going to work together synchronously. However, if too much data is coming in, or if the data is coming in from irrelevant sources, then the binding mechanism will be thrown out of sync.

Imagine observing a firecracker that has both a loud bang and a bright flash. If you experience it close up, you will perceive that bang and the flash as happening at the same time. But how can that be? Because sound travels slower than light, the flash should reach you first, and the sound should reach you later. But you remember the sound and the flash as being simultaneous. Why?

The brain binds the data from an event in a logical way, based on previous experiences, and according to the logic that sensory data arising from an event happened at the same time.

On the other hand, what happens when the senses are faced with widely separated timing between inputs? What if the bang and flash occurred so far away that the flash was obviously seen first and the bang was clearly heard a little later? Why doesn't the mind rectify that? Because logic says that it is too far for the sound to arrive at the same time the flash does.

There is a logic circuit at play when the hippocampus is working to bind the different memories and sensory inputs of an event together. If the sequence of events doesn't seem logical based on past experiences, the experience will seem "off" or "weird," and the hippocampus tends to discard the newly bound memory.

Mindfulness and the "monkey mind"

Becoming overwhelmed by too much chaotic input makes it difficult for the hippocampus to bind memories together correctly. However, if you move at the speed of your memory, that is to say, if you slow things down, and you don't occupy the mind with too many things at once, then you can get a detailed capture of all the things that are going on around you. And that is the art of mindfulness.

Mindfulness is the practice of purposefully focusing the attention with an open and non-judgmental attitude. Focusing on your senses in the here and now is one common approach to being mindful.

To pay attention is to successfully avoid distraction. To avoid distraction requires a solid selection process of what is relevant and what is not. That's the foundation. Being someone who has top memory starts with selecting out what is relevant from what is not, then purposefully paying attention to what is relevant.

If you develop a state of mindfulness in all you do, paying attention to what you are doing and where you are, you will find that the brain is able to remember everything you need it to. The key is to make mindfulness a habit. When you do that, you create the foundation for a stronger memory. In fact, mindfulness is an important ability for an efficient brain, in all it does.

To understand mindfulness, it is helpful to think of your mind as being made up of three parts. The first part of your mind is constantly cycling through thoughts, like a movie that is always playing in your head – a very disconnected and fleeting movie. This is what's often referred to as the "monkey mind" because your thoughts jump around like a bunch of monkeys swinging and leaping erratically from branch to branch.

The second part of your mind is quieter. It goes about its present task, seeking out information and accessing learned skills to accomplish it. This is cognition.

You could call the third part the "umpire." It observes the other two parts and decides what to do. This third part also has a lot of other inputs to take into account – the primitive mind with its basic urges, for instance. The umpire passes its recommendations on to you. ("You" are not your mind.)

Mindfulness occurs when you have aligned the three dimensions of your mind – the monkey, the cognitive side, and the umpire – and they are all aligned in the moment, purposefully paying attention to the same thing, calmly, and with an attitude of acceptance and nonjudgment.

Let's look at common experience, as an example, to illustrate this. Imagine being in a movie theater watching a movie, and your monkey mind, your cognitive mind, and the umpire are all trained on the events on the screen – you are being mindful of the movie. Suddenly, an unruly patron is making a fuss two rows ahead. Your cognitive mind is probably still trying to watch the movie, but your monkey mind has been knocked off its movie-viewing perch and is coming up with all sorts of thoughts about the noisy patron. That gives the umpire two feeds of data – and one is not relevant to the other.

So, now, there are two sources of stimuli: the story on the screen, and the noisy patron. Mindfulness is picking one or the other. It might seem obvious that you should choose the movie, but that is not the point. The point is to pick one, so that all faculties of the mind are trained and focused on that one thing. Which you choose to focus on is really a separate consideration of the benefits you will receive. There are certainly situations where paying attention to the patron might make more sense in the moment.

However, let's assume that you know right off that focusing on the unruly patron will give you nothing but angina, whereas focusing on the movie will give you what you paid for – pleasure. So, you make the choice to return your attention to the movie – but your monkey mind doesn't agree. It wants to continue cussing out the unruly patron.

The question now becomes how to bring the monkey mind back into unified focus with the cognitive mind. Generally, you need to distract the monkey mind with something else. You need to give it something different to attract its attention, because, until you do, it is in the nature of the monkey mind to bring up associated thoughts called up by whatever has caught its attention.

If you wait a minute or two, and there is another exciting scene on the screen, that should be enough to capture the monkey's attention, and it will get back to watching the movie. Otherwise, a good way to do it might be to head out to the concession stand to get a drink and more popcorn. By the time you get back, the monkey will have forgotten all about the earlier distraction.

In a long and roundabout way, this illustration highlights something that you need to understand about the composite mind. Your mind has a variety of functional areas that are each there for a reason and with important roles to play.

The part we have been calling the "monkey mind" is a crucial part of brain and memory functioning, vital to the survival and functioning of the whole being. The apparently chaotic "monkey mind" is the visible outcome of the brain working by association. It is the result of the brain being triggered by an external (or internal) stimulus to identify as many associated memories as possible to relate the new event to something that already exists in the brain.

Associative memory is fundamental to the functioning of your brain. Without it, we would not remember anything. One of its roles is to keep you safe, which is why it is so adept at pulling up negative thoughts and memories. You need the associative part of your mind. If you didn't have it, you would not be able to trigger thoughts based on your external environment.

However, when you need to stay focused and pay attention so that you can remember everything, you need that associative part of your mind to align itself with the other parts of your mind in a single stream of consciousness. If there is a conflict between your cognitive processes and your "monkey mind," then your thinking is not cohesive, and it becomes difficult to keep a memory record of what is going on internally or in the physical world.

Mindfulness brings everything back into focus on one stream. Through regular practice, you attach your thoughts to the things you want them to be associated with. The way you start your day is important. Mindfulness practice is especially powerful in the morning. When you wake up and feed your mind calmness and positive messages, it tends to stay that way for more of the day because the associative function of the brain seeks out related things.

Feeding the monkey with positive stimuli when you wake up makes it easier to stay mindful. Then, even if you do encounter that rude person in the cinema, the monkey isn't going to put up as much of a fuss. So, your first step toward mindfulness is to start your morning off right so that there is more agreement between the monkey, the cognitive mind and the umpire.

You should also keep a check on your mental consumption habits, on what you put into your mind. If it's a lot of garbage, you can't expect to be as sharp as you need to be in order to be mindful and remember things well. Gratuitous violence on TV, video games, and gossip are just some of the unlimited number of things that can affect the associations your mind makes. These are all distractions the mind can do without – and when it does, you will find its ability to be mindful is that much stronger.

The more mindful you can be in any moment, the more you will remember of it. Whether it is a phone number or the nuanced facial tick of a person's nonverbal response as you say something, you will find that with a clear and mindful mind, you will be able to observe and remember more of it.

Practice silencing the monkey mind at least once a day by removing yourself from all external stimuli. During that time, do not look for anything to think about. It isn't a time for you to reflect. It isn't a time for you to ponder or work stuff out. It is a time for you to simply allow the turbulence of your mind to settle down.

Remember that the monkey mind is always reacting to the surroundings – and you do want that sometimes. But, to practice mindfulness, you need to remove the external stimuli and get the mind to calm down on its own. You need to give that monkey a break.

So, as after you drop a pebble into the water in a bucket, ripples will spread outward, then turn at the walls of the bucket to return back inwards, colliding with more outward-moving ripples. The result is a lot of apparent chaos. In the same way, when the monkey is given a stimulus, the ripples in the mind propagate across associated neurons to trigger other thoughts. Those thoughts trigger yet other associations, and it goes on and on. But, if you can stop the original stimulus, eventually you can stop the mind from bouncing up against itself.

That is why you need to choose a quiet spot to allow the mind to settle. When you drop that pebble into the bucket of water, after a while, what happens to the ripples? For a while, they bounce around, interfering with each other, creating some chaos, but then eventually the ripples dissipate, and the water settles down into such a state of calm that you could even see a reflection of yourself in it.

This calm state of mind is the best time to expose it to whatever you want to remember. If it seems like a long way to go to remember something, you are not wrong. It can take time to get the mind to calm down, especially when you haven't practiced it.

There is one more thing you can do, besides secluding yourself, to alleviate the constant barrage of distractions. Simply stop energizing the monkey. How? Don't pay attention to it. When you pay attention to those seemingly random thoughts, you end up fueling them. The more you pay attention, the more the "monkey mind" goes in search of even more associations.

Paying attention to those associations is like dropping more pebbles into the bucket, so that the ripples never really dissipate. Paying attention is like providing resonance to a pendulum in a clock. As long as the resonating mechanism is active, the pendulum will never stop swinging back and forth. With that in mind, then, simply take some time to stop the outside stimuli, and stop giving attention to whatever the monkey mind offers up, and you will find that your thoughts will gradually calm down.

If you have mindfulness practice sessions every day, you will gradually find yourself increasingly able to bring your mind into a calm state. With practice, you will be able to bring your mind to a state of calm quickly, if you start the session by taking three deep cleansing breaths. Do this every day, and, over time, your mind will develop a habit of associating three breaths with a calm mind. Eventually, you will just need to take the three deep cleansing breaths, and your mind will instantly calm and enter a focused and undisturbed state.

In this calm state, it will be easier to remember anything you want. It is the best way to focus the mind, but it takes time to practice. Don't give up.

Breathing and calming the mind has other benefits too. It allows the mind to concentrate at will and increases the power of your mind. But for now, your only interest is to get it to remember.

If you make this calm mindfulness your usual state, you will be surprised at how much better you remember the details and nuances of everything that happens around you. Whether you are in a classroom attending a lecture, or in a conversation with a loved one pouring out their heart to you, whether you are walking through a forest alone, or sitting in a cheering crowd, you will be better able to observe what is important, remember it, and understand it.

Meditation

As much as they are often linked, meditation and mindfulness do very different things. Mindfulness provides the environment to silence the monkey. Meditation is about a completely different dimension of change. Without considering the potential spiritual dimensions of meditation, the physical effects of meditating can be profound. Not only does practicing meditation provide all sorts of overall health benefits, it also

physically changes the functioning of the brain –
and that results in altered thought patterns.

There are many ways you can meditate, but
meditating to improve your memory and ability
to recall can be very simple. It doesn't require any
fancy ritual.

Find a suitable place where you can sit down
without being disturbed. Get comfortable and go
through your mindfulness exercise.

When you feel calm enough, start to focus on the
silence. Do not interact with any sounds or
thoughts that might intrude on or interrupt your
silence. Simply be patient and do not get caught
up with the thoughts or sounds. Continue sitting
there, and just watch all the thoughts as they go
by. Do not react to them. Neither accept them nor
fight them. Do not even give them a second
thought. You can just sit back and allow your
thoughts to settle on their own.

The best way to do this is to imagine watching a
movie. Have you ever ended up being so
engrossed in the movie that you felt that there
was nothing else in the room? You were almost in
the movie. Right? But, then, there's a knock on
the door, and you snap out of your oneness with
the movie, breaking the illusion of being in it.
After you get rid of whoever was at the door, you
return to your movie, but you are no longer in it,
and you are distinctly aware that you and the
movie are separate from each other.

Meditation is like that – in reverse. When you meditate, you actually will yourself to step back from the processes of the mind. You step back and observe the cogitation of the mind and the monkey in the mind. It takes practice, but the benefits are amazing. When you pull yourself back from your thoughts and the activities of your mind, you lift yourself out of "street view" into an "aerial view" of your own thoughts, yourself, and your surroundings – it's like going from a "street view" to an "aerial view" on Google Maps.

The process of meditation, when you pull back from your own consciousness, results in a greater ability to arrange neurons and their connections, and to reduce clutter in the mind. Scientists who have studied the brain with sensors have detected heightened electrical activity in the brain.

But isn't meditation supposed to calm the mind? That seems contradictory, but it isn't. Meditation is not meant to make us placid and calm. Meditation is not a tool to dull the mind. Meditation organizes the activities of the brain, making the mind more clear and alert.

Meditation changes the way you create memories, taking advantage of the neuroplasticity of the brain, realigning neurons in a more organized way, arranging them in groups that are more coherent. That's what you are doing when you step back and watch your mind. Something almost magical happens when you meditate –

which forces the brain to reorganize its neurons and make them more efficient and effective in their connections and clarity. When you meditate, it alters the way your brain makes associations, and, so, your memories become more organized.

How does this help?

When you have random thoughts zipping all over your mind – which is how the associative brain is supposed to work – sometimes, the distraction it creates can be debilitating. Ask anyone who has had to deal with that as part of life. Imagine what a chaotically-arranged mind does to you. Imagine what the associative quality of memories seems like at that point. It can be confusing, frustrating, even debilitating.

To increase your memory skills, quieting these associative bursts will go a long way toward being able to memorize things faster, and binding those memories more effectively.

Meditation helps arrange those neurons (representing bundles and fragments of data) into nice little bundles in ways that you can't physically do. Meditation is like defragging the brain. Have you ever done that on a computer? Defragging basically takes all the files that have become scattered across the hard drive in different sectors and locations, which makes the location of the information incoherent, and rearranges it all so that the information is neatly organized, making the retrieval of information more efficient.

Meditation takes a little time to master, and it takes a little more time to see the benefits. Typically, it takes about six weeks to really notice the benefits, when you will notice a better ability to focus and concentrate. In particular, you will notice that it creates a "silence" as the monkey in the mind becomes less intrusive.

Reflection

Reflection and contemplation helps to clear the cobwebs from your mind and to remove the corrosion that troubles your psyche. The ideal approach to contemplation is simply to ignore the chaos – anything that upsets the monkey.

The key is to center your thoughts on the silence that resides deep within you. All of us have a silent center in our mind. Upon that silence, all noise and chaos are built. When you center on that silence, the mind, cognitive or associative, has nothing to record, the turbulence in the mind begins to calm, creating a conducive environment for powerful insights.

Inside that silence, you will be able to start reflecting on yourself and the resolutions you need to make. Make no mistake, reflection is the only way that you can put to sleep all the ghosts that haunt your mind and distract your efforts for a better memory. Reflection puts to bed all that is unnecessarily vexing your mind and soul, allowing your mind to focus on what you want. That helps you retrieve everything you want to remember. Once you have recorded a memory during a state of mindfulness, all you'll need to do is enter a state of contemplation, and search for the material that you want to ponder.

When you combine mindfulness, meditation, and reflection, you get nothing short of a life-altering change that happens at the seat of decision-making.

Frequency

At its most fundamental level, the brain is a bioelectrical organ. The neurons are constantly sending pulses of electricity that travel rapidly across the brain. That rapid pulsing creates a rhythm – a frequency. This frequency can be measured by the cycles it makes and ranges between 0.5 Hz and 90Hz.

The lower frequencies occur when you are asleep, while the highest are generated during states of excitement. During sleep, your frequency ranges between 0.5 and 4 Hz – that is called the *delta* state. The *theta* state is above that, between 4 and 7 Hz, and is the range of your subconscious mind, the dreamy state you feel under extreme drowsiness.

Just above that is where the best learning and memory creation occurs, the *alpha* state, with frequency ranges between 7 and 12 Hz. This is also where you brain rests in a state of meditation and mindfulness. In the alpha state, memories are encoded with greater accuracy, and they last longer. If you practice meditation on a daily basis, this is the state that you can be perpetually in.

Deeper meditation slows brain frequencies more, falling into the theta state of deep relaxation.

Chapter 9: Fading Memory, Diet, Exercise, and Sleep

In a healthy person with healthy habits, memories fade for one (or both) of two reasons. The first is that the memory wasn't formed strongly enough when it was first created. For example, something may not have been noticed or observed clearly enough to begin with. The second reason is that the memory hasn't been used in a long time and so the connections to that memory have degraded over time.

Those are the "soft" (as in "software") reasons for fading memory, but there are also "hard" (as in "hardware") reasons for memory loss, physical reasons that have to do with chemistry, biology, and physics.

Sometimes forgetting things isn't just about bad memory. Sometimes mini-strokes you aren't even aware of cause neurons to die off. If you find you have really forgotten something, you should retrain your mind to remember it, thereby getting your brain to reconstruct those neurons and connections.

Memory erosion can happen because of bad habits that retard brain activity. If you are not keeping yourself healthy and you have bad habits that keep you in a suboptimal state then you will find that your memory will gradually deteriorate. You will eventually get to a point where it is not easy to encode a memory, and, even when encoded, it won't last long.

Eating and drinking

The more the mind needs to maintain memories, the more energy it takes. Memories do degrade naturally over time. It requires energy to be able to maintain all of them. You will notice that children in poorer neighborhoods have a hard time learning. Poor nutrition is often the culprit. The brain uses a lot of energy and nutrients in forming the memories needed in learning.

If you supply your brain with a constant and stable source of energy, you will find that you are more alert and able to remember more. The best way to improve memory is to eat a diet that provides your brain with the stable energy it thrives on. When your mind is fully energized, the process of creating memories and binding them becomes extremely proficient.

The human species evolved on a diet high in proteins and fats, with a metabolic process that is very different than the average diet of the western world. The human brain evolved to thrive on a diet that relies heavily on using triglycerides (fats) and fatty acids as fuel rather than carbohydrates and glucose.

The point is to feed the brain with energy supplied as 80 percent ketones (a by-product of the metabolism of fat) and 20 percent glucose. To do this, the body needs to start burning fat for fuel instead of glucose or glycogen. This is not as simple as changing your diet; it requires a new way of eating and a few days to change your body's metabolic system. Your best bet is to get on an Intermittent Fast and High Fat Diet. A little bit of research or a book on the subject of ketones will help to understand how you can make that work for you.

Don't forget to drink plenty of water, making sure to maintain a good balance of electrolytes. Being even slightly dehydrated can quickly impair brain function and memory. Water is essential for delivering nutrients and for removing toxins. Drinking more water is quite simply the easiest way to boost the performance of your brain and memory. Electrolytes and salts are important too – remember that a functioning memory depends on the electrical impulses that jump across synapses, something that cannot happen without salt and electrolytes.

Once you have your basic dietary issues taken care of, you need to look at your other habits. Two things that are not good for your brain are substance abuse and mental stress. Mental stress is greatly helped by mindfulness and meditation. Excessive alcohol, drug, and nicotine use can be more challenging, but, to have a strong and precise memory, you need to be able to stay away from those toxins and habits. Small amounts are easily handled by the body, but toxins that remain in the system after long-term use can be a problem. Also, as much as possible, stay away from processed foods, flavor enhancers like MSG, and artificial sweeteners. If you can do all this, you will find your memory starting to get better, and your ability to retain and recall memories will improve.

Working out

The brain is a resource hog and needs lots of oxygen to keep functioning. If you have ever been in an oxygen chamber, you will know how much different it feels to have lots of oxygen.

Some years ago, I participated in some high altitude training at Andrews Air Force Base where they have chambers that simulate high altitude, low-pressure environments. I already knew that lack of oxygen reduces the efficiency of the mind, but the crew teaching the course also demonstrated that, when there is decompression and lack of oxygen, not only do the eyes lose their ability, but the brain fails to recognize that it is not working properly, and descends into a sense of false well-being and silliness. When we put on the oxygen masks, the mental fog lifted in an instant. Only then did we realize that there was any difference. We had not realized what a state of diminished mental ability we had been in. The difference between the state of being oxygen deprived and being in an oxygen-rich environment was pronounced – the brain instantly perked up and was alert once again as soon as we had more oxygen.

Oxygen is the key to increase mental capacity physically, and you should do what you can to increase your oxygen saturation. Generally, we live our lives without any idea whether our oxygen saturation is high or low, but we don't need to don masks to get more oxygen. The best way to increase your oxygen levels, shy of plugging yourself up to an O2 canister, is to work out regularly to increase your pulmonary efficiency and your hemoglobin count. If you work out regularly, at least once a day, you will increase your oxygen intake and blood oxygen levels. That will help your brain function and repair itself if there is an injury you are unaware of. More oxygen will make all the difference to your mental functioning and to your memory.

As a bonus, the endorphins (feel-good neurochemicals) you get from working out are also good for the brain and will keep you in a good state of mind long after you finish the workout session. They will help keep you alert, your mind calm, and your ability to remember in top shape.

Finally, you need to pay more attention to your sleep and wake cycles. Try not going to sleep for 48 hours, and you'll start to feel the psychological and manic effects, and the memory impairments caused by a lack of sleep. Remember, your day doesn't start when you wake up and end when you go to bed. It starts when you fall asleep and it ends when you fall asleep again.

Personalizing your sleep habits to get the right sleep for you is the best way to prepare your mind for better memory, and to have a powerful and active mind. There are three elements to incorporate into your sleep plan for supercharging your powers of retention and recall. The first is to get the right amount of sleep. The second is to get up before dawn. And, finally, it is to have specific routines for the hour before going to sleep and the hour after waking up.

1. The "right" amount of sleep

The "right" amount of sleep varies from one person to the next. There are too many factors to accurately dictate the amount of sleep time you need. But you can discover that for yourself through "experiment." You need to invest in a little effort and record-keeping to discover what your own unique best sleep period should be.

What you are looking for is to wake up without any memory of a dream. Those who wake up in the middle of a dream have not fully completed their sleep cycles. Each of us goes through sleep cycles throughout the night, usually about two sleep cycles. If you finish a full cycle, you feel refreshed and alert. If you wake up in the middle of the first cycle, or even the second, you will feel lethargic and groggy.

Keep a journal to record the time you go to bed and the time you wake up with an alarm clock. Also note whether you have any memory of a dream as soon as you wake up. No need to recount the dream. Markdown these times. Monitor and record the total amount of sleep time you had on the days that you had no memory of a dream – vague dreams don't count.

Experiment with varying amounts of sleep until you have awoken on a number of days with no memories of a dream. Average the number of hours of sleep you got on those days that you didn't recall any dream.

Once you have that average number, then that is what you should aim for as your sleep cycle. Work backward on the clock from 5 a.m. to find the time that you should go to sleep. For example, if you find that you have a seven hour optimal sleep time, then mark off seven hours before 5 a.m. That's 10 p.m. That means you need to start your sleeping ritual by 9 p.m. and then drift off to sleep by 10 p.m.

2. Early to rise

The second item is simple. Get up before the sun and you will find that your day goes really smoothly – it's not luck, it's that your brain is in the right gear for the day and so you are able to handle everything in a way that feels smoother. In fact, many elements that favor early morning rising go into human sleep rhythms, including hormones such as melatonin (which regulates sleep-wake cycles). We have naturally evolved to respond to the bluer light of morning by "waking up" for the day, becoming more alert, with all systems set to "go."

3. Rituals before & after sleep

You want to develop rituals for the start and end of your sleep cycle. These rituals are so that you set yourself into a state that helps you get to sleep. It is the same reason you get your kids into a certain kind of pajamas and go through a series of actions before going to bed – you can't just get them from the TV to bed – they will have poor sleep. You will too. So the hour before you sleep and the hour after you wake up are times that you will do the following ritual.

For your bedtime ritual, choose a specific chair and a specific time. Include breathing and meditation in your bedtime ritual. This time is private and yours alone – it is not a time for chit-chat or conversation. You could also do this as a buddy ritual, with you and your spouse doing this together. Just before you fall asleep, have a glass of water next to you and drink exactly half of it and fall asleep.

When you wake up, start your morning ritual by drinking the remaining half of the glass of water, and sitting in your special chair meditating about the morning, the day ahead, and the things that you are going to observe and remember during the coming day. Affirm to yourself that you are in control, that you are observant, and that you will do whatever it takes to remember. You can add to this another affirmation that you seek first to improve your life, and, after this, you should get to your morning workout.

Having begun your day, refreshed with enough of the right kind of sleep, you will find that you are in top shape to spend your day actively building memories that you can effectively remember whenever you need or want to.

Conclusion

There you have it. By this point, you should have a better appreciation of your brain, the mind that it gives rise to, and the mystery of memory. Memory is at the heart of all the things that you are and do. It is a central feature of everything that makes us human.

This book has given you several different threads that you can pull on to develop your own best strategy for improving your memory and your overall mental functioning.

The brain does three things – it interprets, it processes, and it remembers. External and internal stimuli trigger the need to interpret, process, and then remember. That body of remembered data then exerts influence over new data coming in. As a newborn child, looking at a table didn't immediately result in you knowing that it was a table. You didn't even see what we, as adults, see. It is only over time, as visual memory is recorded, and the features and uses of the table are experienced, that we develop in our memory a profile of the table and what it is used for.

To understand the sheer magnitude of the human memory, imagine a flight data recorder in a commercial jetliner. It records a number of flight parameters in a 90 minute loop. At Time 91, it starts going back over itself to record new data. That data never gets used or accessed unless there is a catastrophe and investigators want to understand what happened. The information includes a cockpit voice recorder that records all communication and sound that occurs in the cabin, plus all the movements of critical flight controls. Flight officials can plug that data into a computer and look at a simulation of what the plane was doing for up to 90 minutes prior to the accident or incident.

That is a lot of data even if it is only 90 minutes. But that is only a miniscule fraction of the data carried in the human brain. We store everything from the moment of the first neuron's creation until death – and we access much of it over and over, at different times, for different reasons, using it in a multitude of different ways.

The brain is the world's largest capacity memory storage unit. The limits of its capacity have not yet been discovered. You can retain everything you are exposed to in one form or another. You have it all there. If you access the memory of what happened in the long-term memory network, you will find that the memory is tinged with the interpretations you made of it back then, prejudices, biases, and all. The brain is no mere data storage device like the plane's black box.

Although we often liken our brain to a computer, it really isn't like one beyond a few over-simplified concepts. Instead, there are quantum devices, logical circuits, and tremendous amounts of back up and associative references in our brain, allowing us to have more robust abilities than any computer or even supercomputer. If you leave the world's most powerful supercomputer turned on, it will stay in that same state forever, but a child will observe and learn. The child will use its memories to create more experiences and test more scenarios, changing itself, its environment, and its own brain in the process.

We have been describing our associative mind as a "monkey in the brain" to the extent that the mind is constantly jumping from one branch to another – and that's just what we are conscious of. In reality, the mind jumps many more times and much faster than we could ever be aware of as it samples every area of the brain in search of the next associated thought. If you were conscious of all that sampling, you would immediately become overwhelmed. The awesome power of our mind and memory is rooted in this constant associative dance in our human brain.

The philosophy behind this book has been to provide you with the understanding you need to improve your memory right here, right now, where you stand. You don't need to take any supplements or concoctions or have any implants put in. All you need to do is to activate the existing internal structures of the brain you already have. It takes desire, and a determination to learn new things, to create new networks of neurons, and even trigger neurogenesis.

That's it. Now, take what you have learned and go make some positive memories. Avoid creating bad memories, and always work to set things right so you won't be haunted by memories or feel afraid to venture down your own memory lanes. If you remember more, and make your memories better, it can change your life.

If you enjoyed learning how to improve your memory, I would be forever grateful if you could leave a review. Reviews are extremely important for authors to help us boost our creditability. It also helps your fellow readers find the books worth reading so make sure to help them out!

.

Printed in Great Britain
by Amazon

79306474R00068